keeping me still
renee emerson

Winter Goose
Publishing

Winter Goose Publishing
2701 Del Paso Road, 130-92
Sacramento, CA 95835

www.wintergoosepublishing.com
Contact Information: info@wintergoosepublishing.com

Keeping Me Still

COPYRIGHT © 2014 by Renee Emerson

First Edition, April 2014

ISBN: 978-1-941058-11-4

Cover Art by Winter Goose Publishing
Typeset by Odyssey Books

Published in the United States of America

for Bryan, Susan, and June

Contents

I.

In Keeping

The storm shook
the windows, gave us
dreams of becoming
other people: I wasn't afraid
to do battle.

In the morning, I felt the glass,
the thin sheet of ice
formed over it. Through this,
I could not discern the outside world
as more than a voice
heard through a wall.

When the voice had no words,
I made my own words.
When the coldness had no home,
I held it in my bones.

When We Started Trying

We begin this tender business, creating
a blood oath between us. In autumn

the orderly growth of summer has collapsed.
Maples become book margins, white

spider limbs from some lightless place.
I speculate my body: graveyard, indefinite

wintering, or apricot sweetness. In the stairwell
we smell other people's dinners. They fill up

the hall as an empty banquet room, no tables,
place settings unfilled. We can take refuge

in the refuge of others, and someone else having
is like us having. A broken arrow toward a remedy,

the dotted line where you sign. You trace my birthmark,
key-shaped, alligator-half-submerged-shaped,

where Grandmother says the angel kissed me.
We plan the future through

breathed-on glass, snow like catalpa flowers,
nature dissembled, blurring what is all around.

Keeping Warm

One could have taken us for a small island.
Under broken windows, we slept with snow
in our hair. Car horns braying,
gaping mouth of our neighbor's parties;
we were borne up on waves. Wool socks,
fleece blankets, your arm across
my chest like a decision we make over
and over again. In the shower,
our feet burned in the water,
skin tinged red as newly made.

With the Thin Blue Line

A mistrust of my body, and I begin to look
for omens. A bat flying in the early morning,
black scribble in the sky.

Two rabbits on the lawn, watching.
The tomato plant ripening
in the husk of mid-November.

The day becomes green,
tornado weather, a stillness
the silence behind museum glass.

My husband says *you're not*,
when he means the other thing.

The rooms are empty,
a coat without buttons.

In the hallway, my footsteps
accompany themselves
like lonely cousins.

Safekeeping

They ground and drank the bones of kings
in Nineveh. Swollen, I too learn *we* and submerge
an ocean, capsule, holy vessel.

Brimming, divided heartbeats like misplaced commas
sectioning the lace of my insides.
Moths, despite the darkness,
batting wings against the pane.

In the examination room, legs propped,
the whitecoats and glasses press
the stethoscope, cold to my belly, and hear nothing.

I make a cat's cradle with the loose ends
of this and do not ask, and do not ask,
until I watch the heart blink back
yes, yes.

Second Child

Nails, grown too long in the womb,
indent half-moons on my skin,
like a place a dog tested its teeth.

Even newborn, the baby grasps
my finger hard enough to hurt.
She wakes gumming the air.

You have a sister now, we tell our oldest,
you are a sister. At two years old,
an external force has changed her
identity for the first time.

The sky tears open, a paper sack,
and beats upon the sterile window
of the cramped and cream-colored
hospital room.

I feel separate from her, like a Victorian woman
I saw in a painting once, with a small girl,
a little off from touching,
the relationship indeterminable.

The baby cries from the everyday pain
of living. She doesn't understand hunger,
but feels it. Her elder sister holds
the bottle to her puckered mouth. Already

the oldest tries on the role of mother.
Because she has less need, she must
need less.

The baby's hair curls damp
with sweat formed between
my chest and her cheek. Curls
like overgrown tendrils of ivy.

Ascension

The blue wildflowers break
underfoot; a first frost, winter's ritual.
I spend my days at the farmhouse.
Always the sound of cows;
at night, the dreams of cows.

Their paths through the grass,
the way they watch
when we walk in the yard.

At church the other women
say I should know, by now,
my baby's differing cries.
That I should be well-versed
in the language of need.

A line of geese moves
through the blank repetition
of pasture. Modest as nuns.
Finally, one rises to flare its wings.

A Pleading Sound

Last night coyotes hunted in the pastures
surrounding our farmhouse, monotonous
like the single-colored eye. It is
advent season, just warm enough
not to snow, typical of this region
in Kentucky where "almost"
twins any story of success. You could
just hear them over the straight-line winds
that scythed the fields, indifferent
to our home, where, for the third time,
the back door was torn from the porch,
the metal hinge an awkward angle.
In my sleep, I asked you about the baby
crying. Coyotes mistaken for human supplication.

Sermon Notes

After church, hanging up our nice
and modest things, going back
between the sheets, bodies
cupped to each other, secure
in drowsiness, as if the day
had never started, as if we
were a fixture, the state
everything goes back to,
to begin again.

The pastor says it is harder
for the rich; the pastor says
a camel through the eye
of a needle.

Outside, Sunday persists.
We hear passing cars, people's voices.
The sun through the blinds
travels from this side
of the room to the next,
a slow sweep of light
over cold floorboards.

The Baby Keeps My Place

While eating again in the deep
confusion of what should be
sleeping hours, she uses
her free hand to casually
tear apart the onion-thin
pages of our family Bible,
right at the part where
God saves whom He will.

Keep

The safest place in a stronghold
is called a "keep." Not viable,

they labeled her. The mother could not
keep. She was shown her chances

for subsequent children
like a sequence of days

we all hope to make it
to each calendar year.

A hand smaller than
a fingernail, that precise.

God gave Hezekiah fifteen
more years and denied her days.

We all hoped she'd make it.
A friend says God did not intend.

A friend says God had always planned.
She leaves with less blood, footprints in ink.

What to Wear

A fit and flare, accordion pleats pressed, a dress
for the awful rowing; something lampblack,
Charon-dark, a skirt that flows out like a river,
that never stops like a river, that holds the water
cupped in its hands then through its fingers,
with golden buttons and clasps, color of the coin
you house in the perfect fence of baby teeth; a dress
with shoulders color of soot, back of sable,
waist of onyx, a scalloped hemline, Peter-Pan collar,
sweet and simple curve of another child
who won't grow old. Raven-colored, ink-permanent,
jet-fast, obsidian lace and pinked seams. Church-length,
with a row of covered buttons, hidden closure.

Milkweed

When the fields
were mown down
and the grass eaten thin
by winter, they stood
on the consecrated ground
by the river.

She, in a thin dress
and not shaking,
sleeves folded up
as if she thought
she was expected
to lend a hand

in the burying, to suspend
in the ground what had grown,
suspended in her. In the air,

the intervals of their breathing.
His then hers, white as milkweed,
and as soft.

Hymn of the Music Minister's Wife

Every country church
has a sign out front,
a jutting hitchhiker thumb
on the side of Highway 53.

Diversion from brushed velvet curtain
of stick-straight pines, blushing
Bradford pears. Stark on white:
sermon title, pastor's name, maybe
a quote direct from God.

The deacons count this as witness.
Homeschool girls down the street
change the marquee every week;
their momma says it's her ministry.

I like best the ones that say the devil
is after you; even better,
the ones complete with a Satan
taunting, curved horns and pitchfork,
spry with a hankering for soul.

Sunday night: spaghetti dinner or potluck.
Music minister's tuneless wife, in the foyer
I bounce my baby, my body's own
call and reply, and miss it

as the church stands, heads bowed
for blessing, hands open
to take, just as mine are
closed around fat baby thigh.

When they sing "Just as I Am,"
they're talking about themselves,
as anyone would be,
while Mrs. Pruitt, divorced,
eighty-three, plays the organ
slower each round.

II.

"And in the morning, behold, it was Leah!
And Jacob said to Laban, 'What is this you have done to me?
Did I not serve you for Rachel?'"
—Genesis 29:25

Leah and Rachel

She was always more
beautiful. Mother dressed us
as twins, made it all the more
obvious. Took extra
care with the ribbons
in my hair each morning, tried,
sometimes, I think. *Beautiful girls*
the women in church
would say, watching her,
brushing their hands to her head
as they passed. The veil
that covered her face covered mine.

Close to One Another

1.

Mother writes to say she wishes
our family were closer,
which is to wish that all of us
were different.

She likes to tell stories
of the times we hurt each other.
A hand curled into a fist.

Stories about the past are the best
to tell. They make the present
luminescent, white with agreement.

What was done ten years ago
was ten years ago. What is done
now is who we are.

2.

Another summer in the mountains.
Cabins built intrusively close
to one another. Yards dense with trees,
pines and oak roots on the trails,
magnolias flowering.

Black bears on the road.
Minivans with storage bins
dug into their roofs like ticks.

The bears: dumb, docile,
replicated in cotton
in the gift shops in town.

Years later, there were stories.
Girls dragged away by their thin,
eight-year-old limbs.

3.

Coffee and oranges
in the morning. Your failed
casserole, whole in the sink.

The end of the summer,
already in the long glide
toward September.

You claim you've learned things since then.
You tell me that Mother knows all
your secrets, and you know all hers.

Hair pulled back from your face,
freckles where once I traced
the constellations in pen.

4.

Heat comes reluctant
through the fanned-out leaves
of summer.

An indistinct pattern over the road,
haze in the sunlight.

Our neighbor mows the grass,
maneuvering between the broken
antique car, child's carousel,
the old stove, knobs missing.

A landscape he'll get to, when
he has the time.

In our yard: morning glory,
pansies, buttercups. Poison
oak we burned away one year,
a nest of baby rabbits with it.

Together we tend
our simple garden,
gorgeous, inedible.

5.

Mother says you beat me up
when you were thirteen, and that
I deserved it, she's sure.

Father remembers he's thrown
a cup at me once, at my face.

Grandmother says that when we were
together, she watched you
hit me on the head, often.

They tell us now that you are
a perfect daughter.

6.

When we were girls, we learned
our opposites:

The saw and whisk:
one divides, the other combines.

A hammer and spoon:
one flattens, the other builds.

We learned the lesson that
definition follows use.

And, later, this:
there are no two things in this world
that are opposite.

Jacob Takes Both

I am not sure which cup
on the counter is mine; I drank
from each, so I suppose
the answer is "both".

This annoys you, my half-empty
water glasses here and there
in the house. Small oasis or reminder
that people live here, after all.

Your mother says you should have seen them
as a sign of character—that I am a person
who never finishes a thing.

Our house is full of reminders—the children's
toys, unwashed dishes, rumpled beds.
Your work at all of this I've never
understood—I step over the mess with ease.
You tend it like a garden with no harvest.

They say people marry those who are
like their parents, but mother never kept
her hair pulled up every day, like you
can't be bothered to be a woman,

and the only thing your father and I share
is that we both know the key to deceiving
a person is to undermine the messenger.

So the children pull it? The baby clings to you,
the knots of his fists tied to the loose strands
of your hair. Don't let him; as simple as that.

Rain for a week, and you say it becomes
difficult to keep our children content indoors.
Here is my advice: another name for *mother*—
diversion. Maybe for *wife* too.

Rachel Takes Vows

When I came back, Mother bought me a dress she liked except for the flower pin on the cardigan. I had a dress already, but she said I'd been seen in it too many times and I needed that new dress, limp on the hanger. I put my clothes in the dresser, ginger with the broken drawers. I remember once Mother wrapping brownies in a paper towel, setting them on the dresser's yellow corner, and I grabbed a bite and she'd said *do you need that?* And I felt big, not volleyball off-season big but actual big, like a body in the suit of a body, and then I skip dinner because where am I heading with all this tasting? So terrifying to grow, let me get small like a bird that can be cupped in your hands, a goose under your arm, all day your arm around me, keeping me still.

Leah as Witness

I read the days between winter and spring;
they go by ponderous and graceful as great blue whales.

In the ocean I would move as slow and would hear
nothing but the blood-rush in my ears.

I read books of myths, legends, consolations to add
to the untouched library of the mind.

Mother had never told me of the jeopardy
in this: the sound of girls

whispering, the role of witness at school,
with the other children.

The world hung outside my window, a ripe fruit,
a question mark.

So I dreamed I was my sister: an outward version of myself,
practiced in sighing and radiance.

The sumac tree's sighing, the sun's radiance.

Photograph of Sisters

A kiddy-pool pulled up
on the porch, our hair cut boy-short
from the hair-dresser game;

in the grass, with ankles crossed,
mermaids under the sprinkler, water curving
a shell in an open, close, open—

Who played the mother, who played
the queen, the bad guy?

Who was the chased, the caught? How blonde
was her hair in the beginning, how
freckled her skin?

What happened outside the picture, in the house
humming summer,

behind the camera, behind the lens? Who hid
the toy dinosaurs for the game—a few along

the swing-set, a few along
the back-fence, and in the oak-roots,
where nothing can grow.

Leah Plays for Keeps

The summer we were twenty-five, we swam
every day, my expanding belly more magnificent
wrapped in the gossip of a spandex swimsuit.

Mandarin orange, something I'd bought in an attempt
to be pregnant and sexy. We didn't have jobs;
we were what some called reckless, others *living
with enviable abandon* or *true faith*.

Each week I looked forward to July's wild storms.
The gnarled look of the world, muting
of the unbearable sun.

In church the young girls and old women
ran their hands across my stomach,
the globe of a new world compelling
them to reach out, to touch.

The baby thumped his own resilience,
kicked so I could feel it.

Waiting for Jacob

The sumac limbs sag,
the vow of winter already
weighing.

A late dinner, drowsy, shaping bread
on the baking stone.

Yellow squash, onions, carrots,
a roast and small potatoes
slow-cooking.

My hands bitter with onions,
apron on, the long soak of waiting
for you to come home.

My self-reliance, old trophy,
what once carried me,

swallowed
in the night's cataract, the moon,

and stars like small umbrellas,
opening.

The Way It Holds You

Eight months pregnant,
I hang a clothesline in the back lawn.
In the nursery window, a garden spider
embraces its tightwoven prey. Anonymous
in gauze-white. Moth, horsefly,
creature that thought it had given
wide berth the arcing legs,
the center-poised *X*. They become husk.
My clothespins like the barn swallows,
solemn, well-spaced
on the wire between our home
and the distant, unseen next.

Thawing Ground

A cool wind, the final
remark of winter.
White azaleas
in the half-light lull
of the evening.
The linden trees shudder.
I wrap my coat tight
against the swell
of my belly and think
to next year's spring
when our child will feel
for the first time
the warmth the world
can carry, and, afterward,
its long withholding.

Leah Speaks Her Piece

I show our sons what it is
to be a good wife, my rights
sunk into caring for them.
I turn my cow-eyes to errands,
to the full sink, the laundry bin.

You were too young, too drunk
at our wedding. The whites
of my veil, my eyes, were gauze.
They obscured, and you took me.
You were mistaken.

I advocate our wedded bliss.
I keep our courtship relics.

She tells me the difference
between annulment and divorce;
she says you will make my children
illegitimate. You'll make it
as if it never happened, before God.

How nice to share a thing, it makes us
like sisters, I told her once.

Our floors are smooth as pomegranates,
and the plates gleam like sheep, each
perfect, with its mate.

Dishwashing

The tedious caress of milk-rimmed
cups, ceramic bowls with sweet skin
of grapefruit juice and honey.

In the cupboards they become orderly,
diaries on a bookshelf, a spine of years.

My hands in the dishwater, thin
with loose gold bands.

Mug

Moon-mouthed, I am
of a set. On the shelf, orderly
as sisters in church.

Each bone-white, handled,
an eye held open,
to be filled. Chosen,

poured into, lips meet
my rim. I brim,
a hand around me,
through me, and I hold
what I am given.

Offering up my sweet
entirety. Until emptied again,

submerged, taken
to a dish towel's
efficient caress.

It Is Well

Once I thought the weather
would never change. Memory
comes back. Expands
and widens. We push
the borrowed twin beds
together, and at night
a leg or arm slides
into the gap, becomes numb
and separate from the body
like a criticism between lovers.
I was told I was weightless
to him. Sunlight on the shoulder.
I do not want to be left
a little at a time,
like streets abandoned
to darkness. A wall
painted the neutral colors
of milk, bread, held solid
by pictures of friends,
family, familiar people
in street clothes, in
hand-me-downs. When they left,
I kept them out. I did
not notice the tattered couch,
the sharp edges
of furniture. I left behind
uncomfortable keepsakes.

They are still here, as graceful as
the arc of waves in the ocean,
and as endless. The awful rowing.

Rachel Sets Up House

You appraise worth with one eye closed, and at night we are in bed
with both eyes open. Men cart in the mattress and cherry bedposts,
the cheap legs of the desk where I do my writing scrape against the
doorframe; the green easy chair we bought at a yard sale blockades
the stairwell. These men are friends of your drunk, firework-selling
uncle, not professionals; their faces darkened with beards, sticky
with sweat. They take off their beer-label baseball hats to smear their
foreheads with their forearms. Left with boxes stacked on boxes,
I sit at the foot of a cardboard tower, as a giant that might bring
destruction; you sprawl on the carpet, arms spread like Gulliver,
waiting to be destroyed, and look at the boxes on our sofa as art you
don't understand. The day brings the unboxing. Your uneven cups
and bowls made by student potters, striped dishrags, tablecloths, the
wooden antler lamp, winter clothes and summer clothes, church shoes
and work shoes, finally equal. I unpack my jewelry, Grandma Pruett's
squirrel brooch; you unpack Jules Verne and Asimov. The house is
filled with us, everything that belongs. The pantry full of canned
vegetables, soap in the filmy porcelain shower ledge, plates wedged
together on the kitchen shelves. Us, in bed with your arms around me,
our only empty place.

Leah Recites a Psalm

Pelican mothers tear out their own
stomachs for their young

when the sea is a mirror
in an abandoned home.
The sea an eye that doesn't turn.

She takes from her inmost
for her children to consume.

You are tired of this conversation;
you tell me that no one is asking that of me.

Those raw, minute portions.

But there is something in love
that calls for blood.

Upkeep

In the blue gray of tornado weather
a blackbird left loose feathers on the pane
of the sunroom window. A smear of blood
like an atonement.

Painting our sons' room,
I marry the color to the rim
because gaps are flaws
we will always see.

I think of the blood spread
across the doors of the Israelites.
A symbol of shame, covered.

You compare shame to furniture,
And it is useful in that way.
To create barriers in an open room
To give you a place to curl up.

A Small Bone, Broken

Depressions from a hard rain
dipped into the mud. The new
buds on the oaks, surprising
as cat eyes, prosper over all
of winter's faults

while still December flickers
in the margins of my mind:
a black stone, black stone.
Feels like a bone broken
in another person's arm.

In the backyard, I see the snake
coiled loosely in the garden,
like a flourish on a foreign word.

Already the birds have begun to call
in the mornings with lungs full of south of here.
Already comes the time to dig yourself out.

Leah Separates

A late frost came in
with this weather; the early blooming
daffodils bow their sweet spring
brilliance a final time as we do
in daily prayer.

Our hands clasped together,
our own hand to our own hand.

There is no one here to tell you
to go to bed, to keep the sink clear,
floors scrubbed. My body is tired;
it forgets that it loves you.

Now the sun skims the horizon,
a tongue to a wafer; now the bedroom
dresses in the uniform gray
of every evening.

What was it that you would say
at the close of every meal?
Thank God for what we have received.

III.

Cicada Shell

My husband and I never cut the grass
where the yard is fenced at an angle;
the willow drags its lines to the ground,
ropes for all manner of poisonous
creatures. I found a cicada shell there
clinging, a crusted shadow.

Breath of amber, popcorn kernel,
cicada shell, I'd keep you
in a box, I'd wear you around my neck,
a wire strung through your hollow head
if you weren't too gross to touch.
On my collarbone, little clinger, you
could be twenty-two summers of the fade, grow, fade

of buzz in the trees Mother used to tell us
was the way the maples said Karen, Lauren, and I
should quit our talking and head inside
for bed. I remember this,
or I read this in a story: I'd climb up
the tree like a staircase,
hunting for the gaps where the sound came out,
then turn from the trunk and look
over the chain link fences that hid
our nothing from everyone else's nothing,

then over the hedged places, then roofs
of houses, then muddle of forest, a dark
wall. Night came, and I'd abandon searching,
step down the branches, listen as the sound
filled the empty limbs; the hum
followed my descending.

Keeping House

We bought the home on the hill for the wooded lot,
the stream in the dip between
rising and lowering land, the pine needle
coat on the lawn. Easy upkeep. Magnolias and firs
blended in a light-refracting canopy, close as sisters
who give their children the same names.

In the spring, it grew enclosed with dogwoods
holding out their white flowers, open hands,
the four corners of the cross, red stigmata
pricking each petal. For me, to stay
was another fear, a fever that won't break;
a wish for a gardener's knowledge
of the earth, pleasure in seasonal routine.

When I was pregnant, I was warned of the desire
for soil; I was told stories of women, ravenous,
spooning it up, pining for the metallic crust
of dirt in their teeth. We look for reliability
for an address that won't change. We paint our name
across the mailbox, above the number and the street.

Ravenous

"The desire grew day by day, and just because she knew she couldn't
possibly get any, she pined away and became quite pale and wretched."
—*Rapunzel*, The Brothers Grimm

It began in the garden, like all sins.
My plum-colored rampion craned
its petals, dwarfed flames curdling
your mother's heart. I envied the arch
of her belly, full yet ravenous,
as she looked down from her window
at me, working my hands in the dirt.

Anything I had, I had to tend carefully;
still, things were taken from me.
Your father pulled the rampion
at the roots, ground stubs into mud;
the earth would not open again.
They call me *witch* because I build walls
around what is mine.

Now a man runs his hands over the seamless
tower made to hem you in. He pries for yield.
A prince pulls at your roots, golden hair
twisted in his fists like a bridled mare.

I thought your mother's folly would have taught you
to beware cravings. When your desire is fulfilled,
doesn't wanting, that hollowness, become what you miss?

The Peach and the Pit

The first time I thought I could die,
I was young and sitting on the exposed
roots of a maple tree eating a peach,

the kind you can only find late
in the season, that holds summer
beneath its skin, and when you eat it,

you hold the summer until the taste
fades and August fades. A peach so ripe
that given another day,

it would rot. From the roots
and shade, I watched our black
Labrador lull in the sunshine,

lay down her head, resign her eyes.
If I had touched her, she would have felt
like the tar bubbling on the street,

less firm, less aware of me. A ladybug
staggered across my hand, no pinnacle
from which to spread red-shelled wings

like Dorothy taps red shoes. I turned
the pit over in my mouth, scraping the last
of the pulp from the wood.

The ladybug flew, the pit slipped
down my throat and caught,
its new harbor. I think about this

every time I eat a peach. Every
time the skin flushes,
the juice runs over

my fingers like sunlight
runs over the hills each
morning, each morning

that I don't die of my
greed, my youth, my
inexorable hunger.

Discipline

I tell my daughter *Do not use me as a ladder*
in Mother's way. Stern, dry as autumn,

a music that slips identity. I learned by rote
the second-hand intonations, the chant
of *do not, do not* a chain through the tongue

how many generations. Cornelia, whom I met
and have never met, a ghost-woman, great grand

German immigrant, pregnant, versed us
in her dialect of consequence. I earned it

young, palm-sting against my cheek, Mother's
toothmarks in my ear, a blood name retuning

my mouth to another thin seam. I tell my daughter
not to use the ladder, climb backward how many
generations meeting in the first words I heard

as a daughter. Made of echoes, arcs, and dips of sound,
blocks I stack together while she pulls them down.

Keeping in Touch

Sundays we write impersonally
to people who used to know us.
You type in decisive punches;
I know the keys without looking.
Not memorization of form
but movement. Correct pattern,
correct words. I dig my claws in,
pull out loose threads.

Family Business

A summer of sifting ashes
for the fillings and bits
of bone, you put on the suit
your grandfather bought you
for a season of sweating
in close-packed Arkansas air.

Always *Amazing Grace* and *the dead
shall rise first*. Chiggers in the grass,
mosquitoes through cotton.
Lipstick across stiff lips,
slipping arms into sleeves.

The quiet something like the quiet
of an unused room.

It was the summer before you married
me. At home, in Tennessee, I wondered
if I'd be easy to live with.

Your Old Home

Seven deer on the lawn
in Arkansas, mid-summer.

Honeysuckle and rainwater.
Dragonflies, coupled,
ornamenting the field.

Once you saw this as an ocean,
the tree a mast, boards nailed
up the trunk, in intervals.

You saw your future there,
and your parents thought you were lying.

We did lie, hide, hold
each other gently, married,
negligent of the old blood
claims to our bodies.

I gave up my name
and you gave up the country.
Still, we come back
from time to time,
to taste, dip our toes in,
keep it as a place we've been.

We Left Behind

Our first teeth, calcium pebbles
in the who-knows-where
of a landfill. Maples we climbed
and the stony soil their roots
run through. Beale, Macon,
Ecology Loop. Speeding
tickets. Taurus on cinderblocks
on my parents' lawn. The Krogers.
Sweet tea and lemon. Fried chicken,
okra. Mothers-in-law. Reckons
and y'alls. Unused wedding
gifts: twelve pieces of china,
a wall clock with off-rhythm pendulum.
My boxes of second-hand
books. The dresser my father built
and I painted blue. Our black
cat who killed squirrels and birds,
the copperhead. Garden flowers drooped
like golden bells and sticker bushes
beneath each windowsill. An outdoor grill
ashy with coal. The push
lawnmower. A house near the river.
The cotton fields tilled
and phosphorous in blossom.
Minnows, bread crust, green waters.

Moving North

1.

We learn an empty house,
the look of a room as a cavity
to be filled. We learn to portion
and take everything to keep,
in labeled boxes that make
angles and a jigsaw fit.

2.

In the story, the sisters cut portions
from their feet, to fit
the shoe. The prince knew
when the blood seeped
over the bridge of the foot,
down the pointed heel.

3.

Cushion wedding
dishes with winter
sweaters, cradle picture frames
with newspaper, perfumes
with plastic bags.

Nothing will break.
It will all fit.

4.

In the Smokies, vacationing
and young, we ate
at a catfish place where you
catch and kill from a pool.

Walking in, my sister's shoe
(She was walking in
my shoes, that did not fit) fell
in the water. My sisters
held my heels, and I reached,
belly in the slime of the concrete bank,
and I pulled her shoe from the waters.

5.

The boxes shift in the back.
The rear window, obscured.
The sun, obscured by clouds
rolling in from the north.

Easter Day

Day of lilies,
day burial clothes lay empty.

On road cut through mountain
we talk a little easier,
side to side, looking
at what we're moving toward.

I've become a valley of dry bones,
the dust in the dust;
I've become a fig tree, withered.

A matter of geography,
of leaving something
in one place and moving
toward another.

Once our future was held as a bird
in the hand.

Wings and a flutter
against the palms.

Cut rock, roots exposed.
Sky the inside of a bowl,
wiped clean.

New Tenants

A red stain beneath the dresser,
like the wrong shutter speed, tells
of mistakes that were made here before.
All our boxes emptied and pried apart,
tape stripped off, laid flat. Unpacked,
we pound nail holes in fresh paint.

Pictures of us at occasions—
white church steeple, blue sky.
Carefully arranged in the hallway,
guest room, over our bed.

It makes all the difference
to see, at every turn,
a familiar face.

Letter from an Occupant

1.

Ambulance siren, the crying city baby,
undertones of the pavement and building:
this isn't where you're coming from,
this isn't where you're going.

2.

Flowered drapes, projector stand,
hair on the bathroom tile, a tension
rod, broken panes in the windows:
what the previous tenant left behind.

3.

The pond on Main reflects the sky, confessing
all it has and hasn't seen.
The maples grow carefully, so as not to brush
dead leaf to dead leaf.

Brownstones hunched together
neck-tied by streets, cemeteries
for sight-seeing, window glass wavering
down the frames. A coming
cold, thrummed into me.

4.

Constructing furniture
from a box: my arms, hands
are not strong enough to wedge
the angles flush.

5.

The tiles and angles do not always meet—
they gap, as a missing tooth, missing eye,
that craves filling.

I worry an item of value will slip
into the unreachable darkness: wedding ring,
letter, photographs of dead relatives. Items
I take precautions to keep.

6.

Phone conversation:
What will you do if there is a burglary?
Call the police, climb out a window.
What will you do if the gas leaks?
Call the fire department, open a window.
What will you do if there is a fire?
Burn.

7.

Formal Complaint:
To Manager, to Landlord, to Whom it Concerns:
The right window in the bedroom has Saran Wrap taped
over the missing pieces of the pane. The wind sucks it in
and out, like an artificial lung, the sound of a woman

rummaging in the grocery sack for a receipt to spit gum inside.
Could this be fixed before my in-laws visit?
Sincerely,

8.

The small town parade drums
and trumpets, high-schoolers
through the main street.
From our home, we hear it, mistakable
for mowing, for rolling a dumpster
down the driveway. The drums,
clarinets, the neighbors grouped
on street corners. They fawn, and wave.

9.

The ash scent drifts through the grates.
Cigarette smoke from another tenant.
The smell of burnt and burning.

Winter Advice

You leave me a note of advice
to layer up and to not take naps
outside—I'll die. But not even
the street people are napping
outside nowadays. They've stranded
their Stop-and-Shop carts
in the snowdrifts, to be covered
and recovered with the snow plow's
push. In melt and freeze, the sidewalk
glasses, the grass silks, the pond turns
a cold-bald face to the sky, and you
coming home is something like a song,
snow heavy in the boughs.

Love Notes

At home, they're sitting in lawn chairs, satellites
to the tin basket the dad builds fires in
every fall night—

the lightning bugs blinking *yes-no*
in the cluster of peach trees
just beyond the wide skirt of the porch light,
branches contorted old man fingers,
no fruit in springtime, leafless early.

Mosquitoes touch here and there;
the flames coax the sisters closer
to scrape ash from the logs,

flick up sparks, red love notes
to a blank heaven.
I would like to read them,
to pick up a stick from the crabgrass.

The First Night in a New House

The cricket song lures
the night closer still:
darkness crowds the porch
light, flickering from Luna
moths, gnats and flies.

You and I are in the hammock
looking through the limbs
of pine trees at the empty city sky,
enveloped in the thickness of the air.

The moon hangs above our house
a mimosa-colored omen,
or a new catechism.
I never understood its orbit—
the waxing and waning,
dark Maria, light Terrae

and even now I can't seem to see
how God's thumbnail, a celestial
body, can revolve around us,
just people, swinging above
patches of forgotten August grass.

The Pit and the Peach

The Grand Canyon, 1990, lobbing rocks
off the drop. His mother's hands
on his shoulders, her worry
of feet slipping. He understood
that every death is your own, every
witnessed near-miss, nail-mark
frantic on the coffin-lid.
I learned it a different way: peach pit caught
in the safe-keeping of my throat,
the minute of panic, knowing
the clockwork monotony of the body
can stop. That we're two smaller shadows
submerged in another, large
like a pockmarked night sky, each star
unbuttoned to let fall.

Keepsake

Where the chain-link fence meets to hem
our land from theirs, my mother
planted the bulb of an iris
she dug from the wasted
garden of my great-grandmother.

Still a child, I thought it was her grave;
the bulb balanced on her forehead, roots
stitching through the alcoves of her
eyes, crevice of her mouth. The stalk:
hard-toothed enamel, hint of bones
underneath. The flower: color
of communion wine.

She would have never extended
these hands, petals cupped
to catch what comes, soft as her skin
tampering to soil
through decay, the takings
we imagined in the summer nights
in our cool beds, the hum of cicada

stretching on and on. This embalming
I understood, not as her open hand
but open eye—colored, reoccurring.

Tending

My parents are traveling to East Tennessee
to walk black-purple mountains
on trails coated with leaves, ridged
with roots, snaked up
from the soil. I tend their garden
of eggplants and cherry tomatoes
that necklace and sag the tomato plant's limbs.

Sitting on the back porch, I watch clouds meet
above me and cicadas chorus hallelujah
to the coming storm.

There is the smell of damp and electricity,
grass, earth, and the thunder sounds far off,
a disaster in the next town. The first drops of rain
break from the mass of water welling above.

Storm Front

Rain falls down the chimney,
rattling like bracelets on a bony arm.
The wind sucks out air
from the house, making the sound of fire
where there is no fire.
I am on our red couch writing,
you are in the bedroom sleeping.
If the storm comes, it will come
for us both, writing or sleeping,
so I let you sleep, the better way
to meet fate: with your eyes closed
thinking of something else.

Felling

My neighbor is cutting down the pines
from her land. A hundred years tall, beckoning
the sky, they attract lightning, she says.

They have become a crushing weight, splinter
of wood piercing her heart, death's shadow
on her doorstep. In the June haze, they creak
and sway their last; the paper mill bears its scent
from corner to corner in this town.

The chainsaws chirr, and we watch
from the doorstep. I feel a sudden need
to run my fingers across the day-old bristle
of your face. You tell me you hate to see
the loss of what should be lasting things.

Already our daughter has lost, at a year old,
the sweet dumpling fat of her thighs,
lengthening with movement. Growing
with our second child, I too feel the rhythm
of loss and gain, the surrender of one for another.

The pines are cut down piece by piece.
Our home illuminated
where the sun has never reached,
and we are given a clearer view
of the indifferent vastness of heaven.

Acknowledgements

Thank you to my teachers, especially Maggie Dietz, Louise Glück, Robert Pinsky, and Bobby C. Rogers, for their encouragement and advice in writing these poems. To Heather Cadenhead for her countless poetry critiques, support, and enduring friendship. Sincerest thanks to my parents, Ray and Beth Roberson, and my sisters, Karen and Lauren, for their faith in me. To my muses, my daughters Susan and June. Thanks especially to my husband, Bryan.

Thank you to the editors for the following journals in which these poems first appeared, sometimes under different titles:

2 River Review: "Storm Front"
32 Poems: "What to Wear"
The American Literary Review: "The Peach and the Pit"
Apple Valley Review: "New Tenants" and "With the Thin Blue Line"
Big Muddy: "Sermon Notes"
Boxcar Poetry Review: "When We Started Trying"
The Chimes: "A Small Bone, Broken" and "Thawing Ground"
Christianity and Literature: "Easter Day"
Cider Press Review: "Leah As Witness" and "Ascension"
Crab Creek Review: "Keeping House"
Existere: "We Left Behind"
Front Range Review: "In Keeping"
Indiana Review: "Keeping Warm"
Literary Mama: "The Way It Holds You"
Memoir (and) Journal: "Letter from an Occupant"
Paradigm Shift: "Keeper"
Prick of the Spindle: "A Pleading Sound"

Read This: "Winter Note"
Reed Magazine: "Keepsake"
Relief Magazine: "First Night in a New House"
Rock and Sling: "Felling" and "Leah Speaks Her Piece"
Ruminate Magazine: "Upkeep" and "Moving North"
Southern Humanities Review: "Your Old Home" and "Milkweed"
Stealing Time: "Safekeeping"
Stirring: "It Is Well"
Sweet: "The Pit and the Peach"
Tar River Poetry: "Rachel Sets Up House"
Two Review: "Family Business"
Valley Voices: "Close to One Another" and "Waiting for Jacob"

About the Author

Pushcart Prize nominated poet Renee Emerson is an intensely moving writer whose work is not only immersed in human emotion, but also draws power from hope found in the midst of a fallen and broken world. She earned her MFA in poetry from Boston University, where she was also awarded the Academy of American Poets Prize in 2009. Renee teaches creative writing and composition at Shorter University in Rome, Georgia, where she lives in a little brick house in the woods with her husband and daughters.